Joseph D Fay

Guide to changes in the New York statute law, made since

the year 1858

Adapted to the fifth edition of the Revised statutes

Joseph D Fay

Guide to changes in the New York statute law, made since the year 1858
Adapted to the fifth edition of the Revised statutes

ISBN/EAN: 9783744739504

Printed in Europe, USA, Canada, Australia, Japan

Cover: Foto ©Lupo / pixelio.de

More available books at **www.hansebooks.com**

GUIDE TO CHANGES

IN THE

NEW YORK STATUTE LAW,

MADE SINCE THE YEAR 1858.

ADAPTED TO THE

FIFTH EDITION OF THE REVISED STATUTES,

WITH A REFERENCE TO EACH PAGE AND SECTION OF
SAID EDITION AFFECTED BY SUBSEQUENT LEGISLA-
TION, AND ALSO THE DATE AND CHAPTER OF
THE AMENDATORY ACTS.

BY JOSEPH D. FAY,

COUNSELLOR AT LAW.

NEW YORK:
BAKER, VOORHIS & CO., PUBLISHERS,
66 NASSAU STREET.
1873.

INTRODUCTION.

The Revised Statutes of New York, enacted in 1827 and 1828, were published in 1829. Subsequent legislation introduced so many innovations, that to present at one view, without confusion, the bulk of positive law in force in this State, later editions have been justly considered necessary from time to time. The second, of 1836, and the third, of 1846, were respectively edited by John Duer, Benjamin F. Butler, and John C. Spencer, the original Revisers. To the labors of Hiram Denio and William Tracy, we are indebted for the edition of 1852. The most recent was prepared by Amasa J. Parker, George Wolford and Edward Wade, and was published in 1859.

In 1836, the Revisers wrote, "A new edition of the Revised Statutes seems required by the wants of the citizens of this State. The alterations made by the Legislature are so numerous and important as to create great difficulty in ascertaining the exact state of the statute laws, unless those relating to the same subject are placed together so as to exhibit their mutual relation."

The want of a new collection must be still greater at the present time. Since the excellent work of Judge Parker and his associates, nearly eleven thousand new laws have been passed. To collate these is no trifling labor. No digest exists properly arranging them. The result is that practitioners are subjected to unnecessary exertion and loss of time, in searching through the numerous volumes of session laws; the indices of some of which are far from unfailing guides. Instances are not rare where important clauses of statutes have escaped the attention of astute lawyers and learned and accurate judges.

Former editors reproduced the original text, except when modified by later acts, omitting the portions expressly repealed, adding clauses of subsequent statutes in the appropriate places. To get rid of embarrassments in classification, the sections were renumbered, and additional titles were provided for new topics.

Beside the cancellation of the text in terms, many portions have been abrogated by the sweeping clause in certain acts, repealing those which wholly or partially conflicted. Sometimes later statutes contain provisions necessarily inconsistent with those pre-existing, without referring to them. Occasionally a repealing statute is itself repealed, thus reviving the prior one, as in the case of writs of *certiorari* to courts of Special Sessions.

The destruction and modification of statutes by implication frequently gives rise to questions which can only be settled by adjudications of the court of last resort. In the fifth, as well as former editions, the editors omitted such sections and titles as they deemed abrogated by the force of later acts. In some cases, the courts have differed in opinion from the learned editors. Memoranda of some of these appear in these pages. With the view that counsel would prefer to decide for themselves questions of construction, references are made chronologically to all acts passed on similar subjects since the last revision.

The purpose of this little work is to point out what changes have been made since 1858, in any way affecting the general statutes, as embodied in Judge Parker's edition. The notes are made with reference to each section. The Code of Procedure has not been annotated here, for reasons deemed sufficient. Local laws have not been considered, except such as relate to courts in New York, Kings, and Westchester counties, and to the general functions of public officers in those important portions of the State. An exception has also been made as to the boundaries of towns and the creation of new ones. A few old statutes have been cited, and occasionally a judicial decision, although they are not within the scope of this volume.

Some acts, having general titles, are purely local, as chapter 864, of 1868, entitled " An act to authorize the drainage of marsh land," the operation of which is confined to Staten Island and Long Island. Others, strictly local, contain general provisions, such as the Metropolitan Police law, which authorized the execution by the district officers of criminal warrants throughout the State, without backing.

Every statute passed since 1858, up to the close of the last session, has been carefully examined and assigned to its appropriate position. The magnitude of this labor may be judged by considering the contents of the volumes of Session Laws, which, from 1859 to 1872, both inclusive, embrace 9,992 chapters.

These notes may be written in the margin of the Fifth Edition of the Revised Statutes, opposite the section or subdivision indicated on the left hand side. When the statute cited affects an entire title, or a considerable part of it, the reference is to be written opposite the syllabus or head note of the title. When a cited act is on a new topic, the note is to be written either at the top or bottom of a page, where subjects somewhat analogous are treated of, or is to be placed in the general index at the end of Vol. III.

The present writer, while a student, was led, for his own convenience, to make classified references to the session laws. These having been found serviceable, were afterwards continued.

The manuscript notes were submitted to Charles O'Conor, Esq., who, in a private letter, dated July 28th, 1871, wrote, "Such a performance, if conducted with strict accuracy, is of a useful nature. It certainly would be a service that all of us might desire, provided the annotations could be relied upon as complete." After pointing out a few of the apparent defects, that distinguished lawyer concluded, "You must not think me an unfriendly critic. So far as I may seem censorious, you will, I hope, esteem it as evincing only a desire to aid you in making perfect the useful work you have commenced."

The annotations have since been thoroughly revised and the references verified.

A member of the bar of much research was so kind as to observe that these materials should be made public, for the use of the profession. The plan of this work has been since approved, and the importance of its object acknowledged by ex-Judge John Kerr Porter and Chief Judge Charles P. Daly, and other eminent members of the profession.

JOSEPH D. FAY.

Aprıl 4th, 1873.

AMENDMENTS

TO THE

FIFTH EDITION OF THE REVISED STATUTES,

VOL. I.

PAGE.   SECTION.

217,   Subdivision   2...1859, ch. 515 ; 1860, ch. 200.

"   "   3...   "   "

"   Foot of page....Indian Lake, 1859, ch. 515 ; 1860, ch. 200.

218,   Subdivision   4...1860, ch. 200 ; 1862, ch. 491.

"   "   5...1862, ch. 491 ; 1860, ch. 200.

"   "   6...1859, ch. 515 ; 1860, ch. 200 ; 1862, ch. 491.

219,   22............1859, ch. 515 ; abolished 1860, ch. 200.

224,   Subdivision   2...1861, ch. 341.

"   "   3...1861, ch. 342.

"   "   4...1871, ch. 950.

226,   "   9...1871, ch. 949.

227,   "   12...1861, chs. 341, 342 ; 1862, ch. 492 ; 1871, ch. 949.

"   "   13...1862, ch. 492.

"   "   14...1871, ch. 950.

234,   Foot of page....Waddington, 1860, ch. 527.

"   "   Clifton, 1868, ch. 270.

236,   19............1868, ch. 270.

241,   Subdivision 14...(Stark ?), 1869, ch. 922 ; 1870, ch. 811.

"   Subdivision 15...1870, ch. 811.

"   "   17...1869, ch. 922.

242,   "   1...1867, ch. 351.

"   "   3...(Boonville ?) ; 1867, ch. 352.

243,   Foot of page....Forestport, 1871, ch. 947.

244,   Subdivision 10...1867, ch. 351.

245,   "   13...1871, ch. 947.

247,   "   26...1867, ch. 352.

254,   "   13...1868, ch. 882.

255,   "   15...1868, ch. 882.

266,   Subdivision 17...1859, ch. 514.

267,   "   24...   "

273,   "   2...1863, ch. 516.

"   "   3...Changed to Fenton, 1867, ch. 158.

275,   "   9...1863, ch. 516.

"   Foot of page....Conklin & Kirkwood, 1860, ch. 526.

277,   "   ....Cuyler, 1859, ch. 517.

282,   Subdivision 3...1867, ch. 795.

"   "   5...   "

PAGE. SECTION.

408, 8 .... Salary of clk. and deputy clk. of Oyer & T. in N. Y. 1869, ch. 599.

414, 51 .... 1866, ch. 629.

416, 61 .... Or by legislature, 1867, ch. 335.

417, Top of page .... Actions against public officers, &c., to protect local public property, 1872, ch. 161.

418, Title I, head n ... Registry act, 1859, ch. 380 ; 1861, ch. 307; 1865, ch. 740; 1866, ch. 812; repealed except as to N. Y. city, 1870, ch. 503.

Registry act, excepting N.Y. & Brklyn. 1872, ch. 570.

Registry, N. Y. city, 1872, ch. 675.

" 1 .... Soldiers' vote, 1864, chs. 9, 253 ; 1865, ch. 570; Rpld. 1866, ch. 524.

" 2 .... Juveniles exempted, 1872, ch. 113.

419, 6, subdivision 3.1872, ch. 698.

422, Top of page .... As to N. Y. city, 1870, ch. 138 ; 1871, ch. 572 ; 1872, ch. 675.

423, 14 .... N. Y. city, 1860, ch. 480.

425, 21 .... Brklyn. 1870, ch. 396.

" Head note ..... As to N. Y. city, 1870, ch. 138 ; 1871, ch. 572 ; 1872, ch. 570.

As to Brklyn. 1872, ch. 575.

427, Top of page .... Voters residing on Indian lands, 1870, ch. 134.

430, 23 .... 1870, ch. 388.

432, 29 .... 1871, ch. 712.

433, 38 .... Misconduct at elections, 1860, ch. 259, § 43.

447, Head note ...... Using fraudulent certificates of naturalization, a felony, 1869, ch. 802.

452, 2 .... 1866, ch. 607.

455, Top of page .... Officers, 1872, chs. 12, 485. .

460, 22 .... 1870, ch. 215.

461, 25 .... 1868, ch. 345; 1871, ch. 184.

" 28 .... 1859, ch. 252; 1869, ch. 831.

462, Head note ...... 1872, ch. 12.

465, Top of page .... Officers and their pay, 1872, chs. 12, 485.

466, 9 .... 1859, ch. 1 ; 1860, ch. 395.

469, 8, 9, 10, 11 ..... Unconstitutional, Ct. of Appeals, 1872.

PAGE.	SECTION.	
469,	15............	*Vide post,* Vol. I, p. 489.
487,	1............	1829, ch. 252.
"	Foot of page....	As to actions against corporations, 1870, ch. 151.
489,	17............	*Vide ante,* 469, § 15.
491,	Head note......	1859, ch. 437; 1870, ch. 113.
495,	Top of page....	Commissioners to examine accounts of State officers, 1862, ch. 223.

Annual reports of State officers, when to be completed, 1859, ch. 437.

498,	21............	1859, ch. 437.
506,	Subdivision 8...	1869, ch. 698.
"	" 9...	"
"	" 10...	"
507,	2d paragraph...	1861, ch. 177.
519,	15............	"
520,	24............	1872, ch. 115.
521,	27............	1861, ch. 177.
541,	Art. 1st, head n..	1869, ch. 196.
576,	22............	1863, ch. 200.
577,	24............	State Museum of Nat. Hist. 1870, ch. 557; 1871, ch. 711.
580,	Top of page.....	When disqualified, auditor to act, 1859, ch. 376.
"	Head note......	1859, ch. 495; 1866, ch. 836.
581,	Top of page.....	To remove encroachments, 1865, ch. 727; 1866, ch. 657.
582,	25............	1870, ch. 222.
584,	36............	1859, ch. 495.
593,	Head note......	1866, ch. 836; 1868, ch. 579; 1870, ch. 321.
601,	Head note......	1859, ch. 495.
608,	"	1862, ch. 169; 1865, ch. 477.
617,	Foot of page....	Asst. Coll'rs abolished, 1859, ch. 495.
621,	Head note......	1861, ch. 124.
623,	242............	1859, ch. 16.
630,	301............	1864, ch. 412.
634,	Head note......	1860, ch. 86; 1864, ch. 252; 1867, ch. 577.

Contract system and contracting board abolished, 1870, ch. 55.

PAGE.   SECTION.

825,   34.............Oath, Const. 1846, art. 12.

826,   43..............1872, ch. 788.

828,   55.............Also excepting poundmasters in West-
        chester county, and certain tax receivers.

"   59.............Repld. as to Ass'rs and Comm'rs of H.
        1845, ch. 180, §§ 2, 4.

"   61.............Poundmasters in Westchester county,
        1857, ch. 447. Justices of P., 1859, ch. 476;
        superseding, 1849, ch. 28. See also Tax Receivers'
        Acts.

"   Note.........Instead of "two justices of the peace,"
        substitute "three justices of the peace and super-
        visor."

"   Foot of page....Inspectors of election, *vide ante*, p. 425.

829,   Art. First, head n.As to schools, *vide post*, Vol. II.

"   1.............He is now to receive school moneys,
        1846, ch. 179.

"   5.............1866, ch. 534.

"   Foot of page....May administer certain oaths, 1870,
        ch. 69. To report town debt, 1870, ch. 552. To
        give bond, 1866, chs. 78, 534; 1868, ch. 721.

830,   Top of page ....To deposit in bank moneys to pay
        town bonds, 1871, ch. 38.

831,   Top of page ....Animals at large on highway, &c.,
        1862, ch. 459; 1867, ch. 814; 1869, ch. 424; 1872,
        ch. 776. Westchester county strays, &c., 1857,
        ch. 447.

833,   30.............1860, ch. 267; 1866, ch. 540; 1871,
        ch. 635; 1872, ch. 377.

"   31.............1866, ch. 540; 1871, ch. 635.

"   32.............   "   "

834,   39.............   "   "

"   43.............   "

"   Art. Fifth, head n.1860, ch. 58; 1863, ch. 172; 1866,
        ch. 832.

                Speedy repair of roads and bridges,
        post, Vol. II, 414; and 1865, ch. 442.

"   Foot of page....To cancel paid town bonds, 1870, ch.
        552. To expend surplus excise moneys, 1872, ch.
        143. May establish free public libraries, 1872, ch.
        458.

835,   Top of page ....As to lands leased in Westchester
        county for non-payment of taxes, 1863, ch. 430.

PAGE.   SECTION.

Not to audit their own accounts, 1869, ch. 855; rpld. by omission from act, 1870, ch. 432. Form of justices' criminal acc'ts, 1869, ch. 855; 1870, ch. 432; 1871, ch. 274. Appeals from justices' bills, 1871, ch. 274.

835,   46 . . . . As to volunteers, 1864, chs. 38, 72, 390.

836,   53 . . . . And justices, 1860, ch. 305; $2, 1870, ch. 242.

"   55 . . . . Westchester county, 1857, ch. 447.

837,   Title VI, head n. Payment of town bonds, 1870, chs. 300, 438.

838,   Top of page . . . . Public officers having town moneys, to report to B'd of Sup'rs, 1863, ch. 404; 1864, ch. 341.

840,   17 . . . . In cities, 1860, ch. 39.

841,   Note . . . . After 1858, ch. 260, insert 1860, ch. 422.

847,   Art. First, head n. Officers receiving fines, or town, city or county moneys, to account annually with B'd of Sup'rs, 1863, ch. 404; 1864, ch. 341.

848,   Foot of page. . . . Westchester county B'd may regulate payment over of taxes by collectors, 1868, ch. 546.

849,   9 . . . . 1871, ch. 18; 1872, ch. 319.

"   Foot of page. . . . To fix disputed town boundary lines, 1870, ch. 361.

850,   Top of page . . . . To legalize informal acts of town meetings and T. officers, and correct clerical errors of T. officers, 1871, ch. 695.

"   10 . . . . '. . As to R. R. debt, 1870, ch. 597.

850,   Foot of page. . . . To regulate tolls on roads, bridges and ferries; repair roads and buy bridges, 1869, ch. 855.

851,   Top of page. . . . . To authorize T. Supervisor to borrow necessary money for repairing and building roads and bridges; town and county soldiers' monuments; to legalize informal acts of towns and town officers, and correct clerical errors in assessments, &c; have charge of records, and cause them to be re-copied when necessary, 1869, ch. 855.

852,   18 . . . . $3 per day and mileage, except New York and Kings, 1869, ch. 855. Salary in Westchester Co., 1866, ch. 609.

854,   28 . . . . 1870, ch. 69.

855,   Top of page. . . . . To fix charges for conveying juvenile delinquents and insane criminals, 1859, ch. 254.

2

PAGE. SECTION.

891, 266 . . . . Except in N. Y. Co., 1870, ch. 752.

892, Top of page . . . . . To sue for certain unpaid county, city or town moneys, 1863, ch. 404.

896, ' 291 . . . . 1863, ch. 362.

900, 313 . . . . Maps to be transferred from county clerk's office, 1871, ch. 106.

902, Top of page . . . . Public officers having county, city, and town moneys, to report to B'd of Sup'rs, and pay over to County Treasurer, 1863, ch. 404; 1864, ch. 341.

903, 4 . . . . 1870, ch. 467; 1872, ch. 767.

" 5 . . . . "   "

" 6 . . . . 1872, ch. 767.

906, Subdivision 4 . . . . 1866, ch. 136.

908, 4 . . . . By county line, 1871, ch. 287; Rpld. 1872, ch. 355.

909, Art. 2d, head n . . To register deaths, 1864, ch. 380; Rpld. 1865, ch. 723.

Adding property omitted and back tax on same, 1865, ch. 453.

Apportioning valuation of R. Rs. among school districts, 1867, ch. 694.

When real estate is divided by boundary of road districts, 1871, ch. 171.

914, Top of page . . . . State equalization, 1859, ch. 312.

" Head note . . . . . . 1865, ch. 453; 1868, ch. 575.

920, 15 . . . . As to Westchester county, 1868, ch. 546.

922, 26 . . . . 1862, ch. 194.

924, Head note . . . . . . Supplementary proceedings, 1867, ch. 361.

R. R. Co's may pay tax direct to County Treasurers, 1870, ch. 506.

928, 61 . . . . 1866, ch. 528.

929, Head note . . . . . . Effect of deeds by County Treasurer and County Judge on tax sales (made under laws of 1850, ch. 298, which was repld. by 1855, ch. 92), 1866, ch. 820.

Supreme Ct. may order land claimed by two or more, to be sold for taxes, or extend the time for redemption six months, 1869, ch. 859. Comptroller not to be interested, 1862, ch. 285.

PAGE.   SECTION.

930,   Head note......1860, ch. 209 ; 1862, ch. 285.

935,   101...........1860, ch. 209.

936,   106.... ....Redemption by mortgagee, 1870, ch. 280.

937,   112...........Notary's fee 75 cents, 1859, ch. 170.

"   113...........1870, ch. 280.   As to Brooklyn, 1860, ch. 158.

"   114...........1870, ch. 280.

"   117...........   "

"   118...........Rpld. 1862, ch. 285 ; and this rpld. 1870, ch. 280.

946,   Foot of page....Taxation of banks, 1863, ch. 240 1866, ch. 761 ; 1867, ch. 861.

947,   Head note......Actions by taxpayers against public officers and agents, 1872, ch. 161.

948,   Top of page.....Action where land divided by county line is wrongly assessed or taxed, 1870, ch. 325.

"   5.............. *Vide* also *ante*, p. 928.

949,   Top of page.....Informal acts of towns and town officers may be legalized, and clerical errors of town officers in assessments, &c., may be corrected by B'ds of Supervisors, 1869, ch. 855 ; 1871, ch. 695.

955,   Art 1st, head n..1859, chs. 295, 302.

959,   23.............1870, ch. 382.

966,   59.............Rpld. 1862, ch. 152.

"   60.............   "   "

"   61.............   "   "

967,   62.............   "   ·"

976,   Head note......1870, ch. 383, §§ 14, 27.

998,   Art. 1st, head n..1870, ch. 221.

1007, 31.............1860, ch. 158.

PAGE. SECTION.

425, 14............As to canal boats, 1871, ch. 205.
426, 19, 2d paragraph.1871, ch. 293.
428, 23............1865, ch. 115 ; 1871, ch. 293.
"   24............1865, ch. 115; 1868, ch. 227; 1871, ch. 293.
429, 26............1860, ch. 64; 1865, ch. 115 ; 1867, ch. 936 ; rpld. 1868, ch. 227.
"   27............1865, ch. 115.
"   28.........:....   "
431, 40............1867, ch. 930.
432, 41............1865, ch. 137; 1867, ch. 311; 1870, ch. 548.
"   42............1865, ch. 137; 1867, ch. 311; 1870, ch. 548.
434, 55............1863, ch. 412; 1865, ch. 712.
"   57............1870, ch. 548.
436, 63............Or to throw dead animals in N. Y. harbor, 1871, ch. 756 ; 1872, ch. 409.
437, 69............Rpld. 1862, ch. 428.
438, 71............1860, ch. 254.
"   74............To be licensed, 1862, ch. 265.
439, 77............As to treas.'s duty, rpld. 1863, ch. 412.
"   78............1863, ch. 412.
447, Head note......1860, chs. 436, 522; 1865, ch. 661.
450,   "   ......1860, ch. 522 ; 1862, ch. 481.
452,   "   ......1867, chs. 256, 945. And Bkln. 1860, ch. 254 ; 1862, ch. 479 ; 1870, ch. 707; 1872, ch. 320. Department of docks, 1870, ch. 383; 1872, ch. 738.
455, Head note......1866, ch. 440, And bills of lading, 1859, ch. 353.
458, Head note......1866, ch. 547; rpld. 1868, ch. 103. Fraud at—in N. Y. and Bkln. and reports of sales of ships, 1871, ch. 515.
459, 5............Sales for benefit of soldiers exempt, 1864, ch. 131.
467, 57............1868, ch. 106.
468, Head note......Bbls. for malt liquors, 1864, ch. 276. Bbls. for apples, pears and potatoes, 1862, ch. 178.
471, Head note......Weighing hay in N. Y. city, 1860, ch. 155.

PAGE.   SECTION.
579,   267............1867, ch. 32.
"   268............Loans, 1863, ch. 315; 1864, ch. 113.
581,   Head note......1859, chs. 236, 365; 1863, ch. 372;
        1866, ch. 348.
589,   Head note......1859, ch. 236; 1865, ch. 476; 1866,
        chs. 348, 564; 1867, chs. 475, 476; 1871, ch. 456.
"   Foot of page....To examine Savings B'ks, 1871, ch.
        693.
594,   Top of page.....In N. Y. city, 1871, ch. 907.
595,   324............1867, ch. 32.
596,   Top of page.....Informalities in incorporating cured,
        1870, ch. 135. May extend their term of charter,
        1867, ch. 937.
597,   Top of page.....Actions by stockholders against officers
        using assets for bribery, &c., 1869, ch. 742. Corp'ns
        may hold real estate in other States, 1872, ch. 146.
598,   Foot of page....Joint Stock Co.'s may hold real estate,
        1867, ch. 289. Joint Stock Co.'s may reduce their
        capital stock, 1868, ch. 290.
599,   Top of page.....Certain corporations may increase their
        capital stock, 1872, ch. 611. Trust and Loan Co.'s
        may invest in municipal bonds, 1868, ch. 480.
        Change of names of certain corp'ns, 1870, ch. 322.
601,   Top of page.....Scientific and eleemosynary institutions
        to report, 1864, ch. 419.
"   11............Library omitted, 1871, ch. 883.
603,   Top of page ....Municipal bonds, 1870, chs. 300, 438.
                Reports of town debt, 1870, ch. 552.
                Municipal aid to R. Rs. 1866, ch. 695;
        1869, ch. 907; 1870, chs. 173, 507, 789; 1871, chs.
        283, 925; 1872, chs. 843, 883.
604,   1..............As to R. Cath. churches, 1863, ch. 45;
        rpld. in effect by 1868, ch. 803.
"   Foot of page....As to recording certificates in Kings
        county, 1872, ch. 534.
                As to recording certificates in Kings
        and N. Y. counties, 1868, ch. 471.
605,   Top of page ....General Synod Ref. Dutch Church,
        passed April 7, 1819; amended, 1869, ch. 171.
"   1..............1868, ch. 803.
606,   3..............Word "male" struck out, 1867, ch.
        656.
609,   9..............1866, ch. 414.

PAGE.   SECTION.

668, Foot of page.... Owners of R. R. bonds may make them non-negotiable, 1871, ch. 84.

"   1.............1872, ch. 829.

671, 12.............1871, ch. 669.

672, 14..............1867, ch. 515.

674, 16.............1864, ch. 582.

676, 21.............1869, ch. 237.

"   22.............1871, ch. 560.

680, 33.............1862, ch. 449 ; 1871, ch. 669.

681, Subdivision 5...1864, ch. 582.

"   "   6...1872, ch. 350.

682, 35.............May be under 21, 1865, ch. 246.

"   36.............Reports of Horse R. Rs. 1867, ch. 906.

686, 37.............1867, ch. 906.

687, 42 ....1867, ch. 49.

"   44.............Unclaimed baggage, 1837, ch. 300.

689, 52.............1871, ch. 560.

690, 55.............Lessees of R. R. to make fences, &c., 1864, ch. 582.

691, Top of page.....Drinking water in cars, 1864, ch. 582.

"   60.............1864, ch. 582.

693, 68.............1872, ch. 843.

701, Top of page ....Costs in suits against municipal corporations, 1859, ch. 262.

"   Head note......General act, 1870, ch. 291 ; 1871, chs. 688, 870. Payment of village bonds, 1870, chs. 300, 438. May have police justice, 1871, ch. 688. May establish free public libraries, 1872, ch. 458.

702, 1.............1871, ch. 688.

704, 11............   "

707, 29.............1861, ch. 178.

709, 38.............1872, ch. 357.

715, Subdivision 21..1862, ch. 281.

720, 85.............As to stray animals, 1872, ch. 776.

724, 105........... *Vide ante,* Vol. II, 717, § 65, and *post,* Vol. III, 696, § 7.

"   106.............Add to end of side note the words "for burial grounds."

"   " ....1864, ch. 117; 1869, ch. 727; 1870, ch. 760 ; 1871, ch. 696; 1872, ch. 696.

PAGE.   SECTION.

726,   Head note......1859, ch. 311; 1860, ch. 116; 1867,
ch. 480; 1871, chs. 95, 697. No rent for meter,
1868, ch. 253.

727,   2............ .1872, ch. 374.

"   3.............   "   "

738,   Head note......1862, ch. 425; 1870, ch. 568. Em-
ployees exempt from militia and jury duty, 1861,
ch. 215; but see 1862, ch. 477.

740,   7..............1870, ch. 491.

741,   13............1867, ch. 871.

742,   Head note......1862, ch. 367; 1867, ch. 574. Fiscal
year, 1861, ch. 326. Statements, 1867, ch. 709.
Extension of charters, 1868, ch. 731.

743,   Head note......1866, ch. 577; 1867, ch. 91.

744,   6.............1861, ch. 334; 1863, ch. 6.

747,   12.............1864, ch. 425.

753,   Top of page.....Foreign Co's. &c. 1871, ch. 888.

"   Head note......1862, ch. 367; 1867, ch. 91. Inland
navigation, 1861, ch. 92. Mutual, 1862, ch. 412.

754,   37.............1862, ch. 367.

755,   39.............   "   "   1863, ch. 242; 1864, ch.
563; 1871, ch. 608.

757,   43.............1862, ch. 367; 1864, ch. 563; 1865,
ch. 199.

758,   45.............When to sell real estate, 1864, ch. 563.

759,   49.............1862, ch. 367; 1867, ch. 442.

760,   50.............1870, ch. 476.

761,   53.............When foreign Co's to make statement,
1865, ch. 199.

762,   54.............1862, chs. 6, 367.

763,   " ....To report, 1861, ch. 334; 1865, ch.
199; 1867, ch. 709.

765,   56.............1862, ch. 367.

767,   Head note......1860, ch. 328; 1862, ch. 300; 1865,
ch. 328; 1866, chs. 298, 525, 785, 843; 1867, ch.
708; 1868, chs. 118, 318, 623; 1869, chs. 404, 634,
829, 902; 1872, ch. 100. L. Ins. Co's may invest
in municipal bonds, 1868, ch. 482.

"   Foot of page....Foreign life Co's to report, 1861, ch.
334. Mutual, 1862, ch. 412.

769,   70.............1866, ch. 525.

774,   81.............1859, ch. 263.

PAGE.   SECTION.

775,   Head note......Rpld. 1862, ch. 347.   1860, ch. 153;
         1861, ch. 80; 1866, ch. 828; 1867, ch. 441; 1872,
         ch. 235.

"   Foot note......Both rpld. but existing companies not
         affected, 1862, ch. 347.

778,   103...........Co's of sister States, 1865, ch. 694.

780,   Foot of page....Homestead Co.'s, 1871, ch. 535; 1872,
         ch. 820.

781,   Top of page.....Loan Co.'s may invest in municipal
         bonds, 1868, ch. 482.

785,   Head note......1867, ch. 509 ; 1870, ch. 773.

791,   Art 1st, head n..1864, ch. 337; 1866, ch. 322; 1867,
         ch. 419.

796,   Head note......1861, ch. 238 ; 1862, ch. 205; 1863,
         ch. 134; 1864, ch. 337; 1865, ch. 691.

810,   Head note...... *Vide* also *post*, Vol. II, 968, § 18.

811,   Top of page.....Stage Coach Co.'s out of N. Y. 1867,
         ch. 974.

816,   Top of page.....Co.'s for recovery of stolen horses, &c.,
         and for insuring against such thefts, 1859, ch. 168.
         Co.'s to prevent horse stealing, 1862, ch. 438; 1870,
         ch. 124.

"   Head note......As to Long Island, 1860, ch. 523.

"   2.............1864, ch. 85.

817,   Top of page.....Records of horse pedigrees, &c. 1872,
         ch. 598.

"   Head note......1859, ch. 36; 1860, ch. 238 ; 1861, ch.
         95; 1862, ch. 284; 1865, ch. 234; 1866, ch. 838;
         1869, ch. 326. Statistics, 1862, ch. 293; rpld. 1869,
         ch. 210.   Fair Co.'s, 1868, ch. 781.

818,   5.............1872, ch. 116.

"   Foot of page....Where no county society, fund to be
         paid to town society, 1869, ch. 167.

824,   Foot of page....Am. Soc'y for Prevention of Cruelty to
         Animals, 1866, ch. 469 ; 1871, ch. 76.

829,   21............1863, ch. 77; 1865, ch. 666.

833,   Foot of page....Special police at Agricultural fairs, &c.
         1859, ch. 36 ; 1862, ch. 284.

834,   Title I, head n...Appeals from county superintendents,
         1872, ch. 38.   Indigent and disabled soldiers and
         sailors, 1872, ch. 873.

837,   8.............1862, ch. 473.

839,   15............1862, ch. 298.

PAGE.	SECTION.	

856, 98.............1870, ch. 424.

877, 202 ....1869, ch. 411; 1870, ch. 431.

879, Top of page.....Juvenile vagrants may be sent to H. of Refuge, N. Y. city, 1860, ch. 241; 1866, ch. 245. Female vagrants in N. Y. city, 1867, ch. 409. Female vagrants and prostitutes in Kings Co., 1872, ch. 845.

" Foot of page....Commitment of vagrants in N. Y., 1871, ch. 607.

882, Foot note.......Before "private," insert the words "public or."

883, Top of page.....Investigation as to treatment of insane persons in asylums, &c., 1864, ch. 418. Discharge of lunatics, 1865, ch. 353; 1867, ch. 343.

" 4.............. *Vide post,* Vol. II, 890, § 37.

885, Top of page.....Asylum at Buffalo, 1869, ch. 414; 1870, chs. 378, 441.

" Head note......1860, ch. 450; 1863, ch. 139; 1867, ch. 595; 1870, ch. 295. Willard Asylum for Chronic Insane Poor, 1865, ch. 342; 1871, ch. 713.

886, 20.............1860, ch. 450.

893, 48.............1869, ch. 895; *vide post,* Vol. II, 894, § 51.

894, 51............. *Vide ante,* Vol. II, 893, § 48.

897, Head note......State asylum at Utica, 1865, ch. 353.

" 70.............1869, ch. 895.

898, Top of page.....Accused acquitted on the ground of insanity, to be confined as lunatics, 1869, ch. 895.

" 73.............1865, ch. 734; 1867, ch. 113.

899, Top of page.....As to females, 1865, ch. 353; 1867, ch. 113.

" 77.............1863, ch. 139; 1869, ch. 895.

" 78............. " "

900, Art. iv, head n..1862, ch. 220; 1867, ch. 739.

" 82.............1859, ch. 129.

901, Foot of page....Drunkards may be committed to asylum for Inebriates N. Y. city, 1864, ch. 141; 1867, ch. 470. Drunkards may be committed to State Inebriate Asylum, 1865, ch. 266.

902, Top of page.....Commitment of drunkards in King's Co., 1867, ch. 843; 1868, ch. 483. Female drunkards in Kings Co., 1872, ch. 845.

4

PAGE.　　SECTION.

903,　Head note......Disorderly children, 1865, ch. 172.

"　　1.............1861, ch. 127.

"　　Foot of page....Abandoning wives or children in Kings
Co., 1869, ch. 811; 1871, ch. 395. Abandoning
wives or children in N. Y. city, Laws of 1833, p.
11, § 7; 1860, ch. 508. Disorderly persons in N.
Y. city my be fined $10 or imprisoned ten days,
besides being held to bail, 1859, ch. 491.

904,　Top of page.....Certain other conduct disorderly in N.
Y. city, 1860, ch. 508, § 20.

"　　Foot of page....Bonds by disorderly persons in Kings
Co., 1869, ch. 811.

905,　Top of page.....Fines for disorderly conduct in N. Y.
to go to N. Y. City Inebriate Asylum, 1867, ch. 470.

908,　Top of page.....Fees of associate, 1862, ch. 372. One
Pol. Just. in N. Y. city, 1860, ch. 508.

915,　47............In name of supt. of poor, in Kings
Co., 1869, ch. 811.

922,　Art i, head note..Certain exhibitions and places of
amusement in cities and villages, 1862, ch. 281.
Licensing theatres, &c. in N. Y. city, 1872, ch. 836.

935,　Foot of page....Advertisements in Sunday papers,
1871, ch. 702. Processions, &c. on Sundays in
cities, 1872, ch. 590.

936,　Top of page.....Sunday exhibitions in N. Y. city,
1860, ch. 501.

"　　68............In Met. Pol. District, 1860, ch. 259,
§ 42. In N. Y. city and Brklyn, 1864, ch. 403.

938,　Top of page.....Clks. of Bds. of Excise to take certain
affdts. and acknowledg'ts, 1862, ch. 161.

"　　Head note.......As to Rockland Co., 1866, ch. 436. In
Met. Pol. District, excepting Westch. Co., 1866, ch.
578; 1867, chs. 77, 889; 1868, ch. 10; this act of
1866 rpld. 1870, ch. 175. Act of 1857 held to apply
to ale and beer, except as to inns, and except as to
Met. Pol. District; ale and beer at least $10, 1869,
ch. 856. General Excise Law, 1870, ch. 175.

"　　Foot of page....Surplus town excise moneys, 1872, ch.
143.

939,　Top of page....Unclaimed baggage, 1837, ch. 300.
Ten per cent. of county excise money to be paid to
State Inebriate Asylum, 1859, ch. 381. Excise
fines to Brooklyn Inebriate Asylum, 1868, ch. 483;
1872, ch. 687.

PAGE. SECTION.

939, 2..............1860, ch. 274.

" Foot of page....Frauds upon or by innkeepers, 1867, ch. 677; 1871, ch. 802.

943, 17.............Except Met. Pol. Dist. 1869, ch. 856.

" 18.............   "   "   "

Indians, 1859, ch. 280.

944, 22.............1860, ch. 259, § 49; 1857, ch. 569, § 21.

948, Top of page....In N. Y. city intoxicated or disorderly persons to be fined $10 or imprisoned ten days, 1859, ch. 491. In N. Y. fines on drunkards to go to N. Y. City Inebriate Asylum, 1867, ch. 470. In Kings Co. fines on drunkards to go to B'kln. Inebriate Asylum, 1868, ch. 483; 1872, ch. 687.

" 40.............1866, ch. 658.

" Head note......Steamer lines to sell R. R. tickets from Albany, &c., 1868, ch. 573.

949, Top of page....Unclaimed baggage on steamboats, 1837, ch. 300.

956, Head note......1862, ch. 474; 1863, ch. 462; 1864, chs. 288, 426; 1866, ch. 813.

" Foot of page....Commrs. of Fisheries, 1868, ch. 285; 1870, ch. 567.

957, Top of page.....Unlawful taking of oysters, 1866, ch. 753; 1872, ch. 483.

" Head note......1867, ch. 898; 1868, chs. 3, 344, 785; 1869, ch. 909; 1871, chs. 721, 831; 1872, chs. 65, 433, 595.

960, 1.............1869, ch. 493.

965, Head note......Travel on bridges, 1862, ch. 354. Wild animals travelling roads, 1862, ch. 112. Animals running at large on highways, 1862, ch. 459; 1867, ch. 814; 1869, ch. 424.

966, 9.............Unclaimed freight on R. Rs. *vide ante*, Vol. II, 687.

973, Tit. xvi, head n..1859, ch. 511; 1860, chs. 186, 384; 1862, ch. 474; 1863, ch. 462; 1864, ch. 426; 1865, ch. 642; 1866, ch. 813; 1867, ch. 898; 1868, ch. 785; 1869, ch. 909; 1871, ch. 721; 1872, chs. 65, 433, 595. Private parks—game and fish, 1871, ch. 831.

974, Head note......1862, ch. 244. As to Ontario Co. 1864, ch. 197; adopted by Westch. Co. Bd. of Suprs.

977, 22............. *Vide* Laws of Supervisors of Westch. Co. 1849; and Laws of 1862, ch. 244; and 1864, ch. 197; adopted by B'd of Sup'rs of Westch. Co.

979,   Foot of page....Duties on brokers' sales, 1866, ch. 547.

983,   Head note......1861, ch. 334; 1862, chs. 6, 367; 1871,
        ch. 888. *Vide* also *ante*, Vol. II, 762.

"   Foot of page....Foreign Co.'s to report, 1861, ch. 334;
        1865, ch. 199; 1867, ch. 709.

986,   9..............1866, ch. 825:

989,   Foot of page....Prevention of fires in N. Y. city, 1871,
        chs. 584, 742. Prevention of fires in B'kln, 1866,
        ch. 858; 1868, ch. 632. Metropolitan fire marshal,
        1868, ch. 563.

990,   9..............Fire marshal, 1871, ch. 584.

"   1..............1860, ch. 103; 1868, ch. 820; 1870,
        ch. 423.

991,   Head'g, top of p.After " &c.," add the words "in Al-
        bany."

995,   Top of page.....Tenement houses in N. Y. and B'klyn,
        1867, ch. 908. Brooklyn buildings, 1866, ch. 858;
        1868, ch. 632.

"   Tit. XXVI, h. n.1862, ch. 356; 1863, ch. 273; 1864,
        ch. 466.

"   Art. 1st, head n..1859, ch. 220; 1860, ch. 470; 1865,
        ch. 263. And storing combustibles, 1866, ch. 873;
        1867, ch. 939; 1868, chs. 533, 634. Combustibles,
        1867, ch. 908; 1871, chs. 584, 742. Storing petro-
        leum, 1865, ch. 773; 1866, ch. 872.

1003,   Head note......1860, ch. 259; 1864, ch. 403; 1866,
        ch. 861; 1867, chs. 806, 956; 1868, ch. 535; 1869,
        chs. 339, 446. To inspect steam boilers, 1862, ch.
        168; 1867, ch. 883. To license boats, 1866, ch. 375.
        Superseded as to N. Y. city, 1870, chs. 137, 383.
        Police to clean streets in N. Y. city, 1872, chs. 677,
        732. Superseded as to Brooklyn, 1870, ch. 136;
        1871, ch. 194; 1872, ch. 363. Superseded as to
        Richmond Co., 1870, ch. 497. Superseded as to
        Yonkers, Westch. Co., 1871, ch. 240.

1004,   2..............1864, ch. 41; 1869, chs. 339, 446.

1009,   11, 12.........As to Kings and Richmond Counties,
        1866, ch. 84.

"   13.............As to B'klyn, 1866, ch. 84.

1017,   Foot of page....§ 61 of the amended Act 'of 1860,
        amended as to N. Y., Kings and Richmond Co.'s,
        1866, ch. 84. Met. Police Life Insurance Fund,
        1868, ch. 535. Life Ins. Fund N. Y. city, 1871, ch.
        126. Police pensions, N. Y. city, 1871, ch. 126.

VOL. III.

PAGE. SECTION.

143, Head note...... Wills made in other States, 1864, ch. 311 ; 1872, ch. 680.

145, 44............1869, ch. 22.

147, 51............Rpld. 1863, ch. 362.

" 52............1863, ch. 362.

" Subdivision 1.... "   "   § 1. On idiots and lunatics, 1872, ch. 693.

150, 71............1871, ch. 603.

155, Top of page..... Applicants not speaking English, 1867, ch. 782.

" 4............1867, ch. 782.

157, Head note.. ....1863, ch. 362. Special admrs. and collectors, 1864, ch. 71.

158, 24............1863, ch. 403.

159, 27............1863, ch. 362 ; 1867, ch. 782.

" 30............Rpld. 1867, ch. 782.

" 31............1863, ch. 403.

160, 32............1863, ch. 362 ; 1867, ch. 782.

" 38............1864, ch. 71 ;   "   "

161, 39............ "   "   "   "

" 40 ....1867, ch. 782.

" 42............1862, ch. 229.

162, 43............1864, ch. 71 ; 1867, ch. 782.

" Head note...... When receiver may be appointed, 1863, ch. 466. Surrogate's power as to concealed effects, 1870, ch. 394. Letters, pending appeals, 1871, ch. 603.

" 45............1863, ch. 466.

163, 47............As to executors, 1862, ch. 229.

" 48............1862, ch. 229.

" 49............ "   "

" 50............ "   "

" 51............ "   "

" 52............ "   "

164, 53............ "   "

" 54............ "   "

" 55............ "   "

167, 71............1871, ch. 859.

168, Foot of page.... Property concealed from exrs. or admrs., 1870, ch. 394.

170, 11............Same to minor child, on death of widow, 1867, ch. 782.

173,   Head note......Releases, 1867, ch. 782.
175,   38.............1868, ch. 594.
"   41.............1859, ch. 261.
178,   Head note......Fees, &c., 1863, ch. 362.   Accounts, 1865, ch. 733.   Costs of accounting, 1867, ch. 782. Trustees and guardians, 1867, ch. 782; 1870, ch. 170; 1871, ch. 482.
"   57.............1859, ch. 261; 1867, ch. 782.
180,   64.............1863, ch. 362.
"   68............   "   "
181,   72.............1866, ch. 115.
182,   76.............As to executors, 1862, ch. 229.
185,   86.............1867, ch. 782.
186,   Head note......1863, ch. 362.   Surplus, 1867, ch. 658; 1870, ch. 170; 1871, ch. 834.
193,   39.............1869, ch. 260; 1872, ch. 92.
194,   45.............1863, ch. 400.
196,   59.............Not after three and four years, 1869, ch. 845.
214,   45.............1866, ch. 802.
215,   Top of page.....In Kings County, 1871, ch. 335.
220,   7.............1860, ch. 322.
221,   2.............1863, ch. 464.
222,   9.............Not by R. R. Co.'s, 1868, ch. 779.
226,   Title I, head n...Husband and wife, witnesses for or against each other in civil cases, 1867, ch. 887.
230,   19.............Registration of deaths, 1864, ch. 380; rpld. 1865, ch. 723.
231,   25.............Metropolitan Board of Health, 1866, ch. 74.
234,   45.............1862, ch. 246.
235,   Subdivision 2...1862, ch. 246.
239,   Head note......1860, ch. 90; 1862, ch. 172.
240,   80.............1866, ch. 656; 1870, ch. 277.
"   81.............1862, ch. 70; 1866, ch. 656.
242,   Head note......Non-resident guardians and wards, 1870, ch. 59.
243,   1.............1862, ch. 72; 1871, ch. 32.
244,   7.............1870, ch. 341; 1871, ch. 708.
"   11.............1871, ch. 482. *Vide ante,* Vol. III, 178, § 57.

PAGE.   SECTION.

248, Art. 1st, head n..1869, ch. 411 ; 1871, ch. 934.

"   Subdivision 1...Not without wife's consent, 1862, ch. 172.

249, Top of page.....Binding by orphan asylums or Homes for indigent children, *ante*, Vol. II, 877, § 202.

252, Head note......1871, ch. 934.

257, Head note......1872, ch. 627.

259, Head note......1870, chs. 86, 203.

"   Foot of page....Crier and two attendants, 1864, ch. 95 ; 1871, ch. 238.

260, Top of page......Preferred causes, 1860, ch. 167 ; 1865, ch. 218 ; 1870, ch. 49 ; 1871, chs. 603, 733.

"   Foot of page....Mandamus appeals, 1859, ch. 174.

262, 35.............1869, ch. 99.

263, Title II, head n..§ 37 in force, 35 Barb. S. C. R. 315 (1861) ; perhaps more of this title, 19 How. Pr. R. 415. § 37 (not in this edition) rpld. 1862, ch. 460 ; again rpld. 1863, ch. 392.

269, Art 4th, head n..After word "Procedure," add "But *vide* Close v. Van Heusen, 6 How. Pr. R. 157."

274, Foot of page....Sales of infants' estates before 1852, confirmed, 1872, ch. 524.

277, Top of page.....1870, chs. 86, 408. Preferred cases, 1860, ch. 167 ; 1865, ch. 218 ; 1870, ch. 49 ; 1871, chs. 603, 733.

"   Head note......Designation of general terms, 1870, ch. 408 ; 1871, ch. 766 ; 1872, ch. 778. Reporter, 1869, ch. 99. Crier 1st district, 1865, ch. 296. Designation of justice to hold special term at chambers, 1st district, 1867, ch. 383.

291, 49.............Shff.'s sales in N. Y. city, 1869, ch. 569.

292, 52............. *Vide ante*, Vol. I, 402.

"   55.............Code of Procedure, § 178.

293, 60.............   "   § 388.

294, Head note......1859, ch. 462 ; 1870, ch. 408.

295, Top of page.....Stenographer, Kings Co., 1870, ch. 606.

296, Top of page ....1870, ch. 137, § 120, which in terms repeals 1853, ch. 352, and 1857, ch. 446, does not abrogate the sections relative to the Ct. of O. and T. *Vide* 47 N. Y. R. 330.

"   10.............Supreme Ct. Judge alone, 1853, ch. 352 ; 1857, ch. 446.

5

PAGE.   SECTION.

296,   11, 2d sentence..1870, ch.,3.   .

297,   16..............May send indictments to other counties, 1859, ch. 462.

"   20.............By Governor, 1870, ch. 408.

299,   30.............. *Vide* also *ante*, Vol. I, 883, § 203.
No other members of the Ct. but Justice of Su-
preme Ct. in N. Y. city, 1853, ch. 352; 1857, ch.
446.

"   31.............By Governor, ch. 408, § 14.

"   32.............   "   "

"   33.............   "   . "

"   34.............   "   "

300,   Head note......After Title V, insert *County Courts.*

"   Head. of Tit. V..After common pleas, add [now county
courts except in N. Y. city].

"   Foot note ......Sessions held by Recorder or City
Judge only, 1853, ch. 352; 1857, ch. 446; or by
Common Pleas Judge, 1870, ch. 354.

301,   Head note......As to sessions and appeals, 1859, ch.
339. Judges of Com. Pleas to file certificates as to
their age, &c.; vacancies in C. P. 1870, ch. 861.
County courts, 1870, ch. 467; Const. new Art. VI,
§ 15. Stenographers in Co. Cts. 1869, ch. 626.
Co. Cts. may enforce judg'ts in favor of dec'd judg't
creditors, 1864, ch. 543.

302,   2..............1861, ch. 8.   P. Jurors in Westch. Co.,
1872, ch. 499.

"   5..............1870, ch. 3.

303,   Top of page....May grant new trials, 1859, ch. 339,
§ 4. Stenographer, 1869, ch. 626.

"   Subdivision 7...What to do when judge or justice is
disqualified, 1861, ch. 96.

304,   14.............1859, ch. 208.

306,   35.............1865, ch. 296; 1866, ch. 588.

307,   41, 42 ....Only by the elected judges.

308,   Top of page ....Practice in Com. Pleas modified by
Code of Procedure, *passim.*

309,   51.............. *Vide post,* 359 note and 671 note.

310,   58.............Only Recorder or City Judge, 1853,
ch. 352; 1857, ch. 446. Or Com. Pleas Judge,
1870, ch. 554.

"   60.............Mayor cannot preside.

PAGE.   SECTION.

362,   Top of page.....Practice and jurisdiction in N. Y. county, 1870, ch. 359. Cl'k, except in N. Y. Co., 1869, ch. 246; *vide* also 1870, ch. 467.

363,   Top of page.....Appeals from surrogate's courts, 1871, ch. 603.

364,   10............Authority of surrogates' cl'ks, 1863, ch. 362.

367,   22............ *Vide post*, 919.

368,   Head note...... *Vide* also 1857, ch. 769, as to special sessions and appeals in criminal cases. Said act was partially repealed, 1859, ch. 339; *vide post*, 1012.

369,   1..............1865, ch. 563; 1866, ch. 409; 1870, chs. 30, 383, § 49; 1871, chs. 302, 438.

"   6..............1865, ch. 563; 1872, ch. 373.

"   Foot of page....Stenographer, interpreter, &c., 1872, ch. 373.

370,   8..............Sentence same as Gen. Sess., 1871, ch. 302.

"   12, 1st sentence.1872, ch. 373.

"   12, 2d   "   ..1865, ch. 563.

371,   13............ *Vide ante*, Vol. III, 369.

376,   Art I, head note.Rules same as Supreme Court, 1862, ch. 484. Jurisdiction, &c., 1862, ch. 484; 1870, ch. 582; 1871, chs. 784, 799, 867. Referees, 1865, ch. 436. Marshal, 1865, ch. 400. Stenographer and interpreter, 1867, ch. 784; 1869, ch. 674. Cl'ks, officers and stenographer, 1872, ch. 438. Cl'ks, 1872, ch. 579. General act, 1872, ch. 629.

"   Foot of page....1831, ch. 300, § 47.

377,   Top of page.....As to unsafe building law, 1867, ch. 939. As to fire law, 1871, ch. 742, § 15. As to chattel liens, 1869, ch. 738.

378,   15............1865, ch. 436.

"   17............1866, ch. 701.

379,   20............1865, ch. 400.

380,   29............1860, ch. 379.

381,   Head note......1862, ch. 389; 1866, ch. 758. Rules, jurisdiction, &c., 1862, ch. 484. Summary proceedings, affid't and return, 1863, ch. 189. Fees, 1864, ch. 308. 8th Dist., 1860, ch. 519; 1866, ch. 217. Interpreters, 1866, ch. 745. 9th Dist., 1869, ch. 377. Non-imp't act, 1831, ch. 300, § 47.

382,   Subd's 3 and 4..1865, ch. 688.

PAGE	SECTION.
382,	Subdivision 6...1860, ch. 300.
385,	48.............1866, ch. 758.
386,	Top of page.....As to unsafe building law, 1867, ch. 939. As to fire law, 1871, ch. 742, § 15. As to chattel liens, 1869, ch. 738.
388,	Line 2.........After " warrant," insert the word "attachment."
389,	Foot of page....When jury of twelve, 1869, ch. 410.
394,	Foot of page....Costs in working women's suits, 1871, ch. 936.
429,	15.............Non-imp't act, 1831, ch. ¸300, §§ 25, 30, 31.
430,	24.............Non-imp't act, 1831, ch. 300, § 35.
433,	42.............1864, ch. 421.
436,	2d foot note.....*Vide* Code of Procedure, § 52.
442,	97.............Code of Procedure, §§ 398, 399.
445,	117............1860, ch. 493.
451,	Art. 12th, head n.1866, ch. 692.
452,	150............[As to constables], 1869, ch. 820.
453,	154............1860, ch. 493; 1861, ch. 11; 1866, ch. 692.
"	155............1860, ch. 493; 1866, ch. 692.
"	Head note......In Bkln. jurisdiction $250, and practice regulated, 1871, ch. 492.
460,	196............Except criminal process in Met. Police District, 1864, ch. 403, § 22.
465,	Head note......None but att'ys to practice in any court in N. Y. city, 1862, ch. 484 ; or in Kings Co. 1862, ch. 53. Att'ys residing in adjoining States may practice in N. Y., 1862, ch. 43; 1866, ch. 175.
"	3.............Const. new Art. VI, § 8.
"	4.............Const. new Art. VI, § 21. As to Marine Ct., 1870, ch. 582.
466,	9.............Const. new Art. VI, § 21.
"	11............. " "
"	12............. " "
467,	21, Side note....Add:—and 3 How. Pr. R. 402.
468,	23.............Obsolete, 1857, ch. 446, § 48.
"	24............. " " "
473,	32.............1859, ch. 360; 1860, ch. 443; 1861, ch. 246 ; 1863, ch. 508.

PAGE.   SECTION.

473,   Foot of page.... Powers of notaries in N. Y. and Kings
            Co's, 1872, ch. 703.

474,   35.............Foreign protests, 1865, ch. 309.

"   38.............District Court Justice, N. Y. city,
            1857, ch. 344, § 77. Marine Court Justices, N. Y.
            city, 1813, ch. 86, § 139.

475,   42.............1860, ch. 276.

477,   Head note......Att'ys residing in other States may
            practice here, 1862, ch. 43; 1866, ch. 175. Admis-
            sion of att'ys, &c., 1871, ch. 486; 1872, ch. 260.

479,   73.............1865, ch. 296; 1866, ch. 588.

480,   Foot of page.... Courts in times of epidemic disease,
            1866, ch. 174.

482,   Head note......THE CHANGES IN THE CODE OF PROCEDURE
            HAVE BEEN TOO NUMEROUS TO BE INDICATED IN THIS
            WORK.

589,   4.............1870, ch. 78.

590,   2............. *Vide* also Code of Procedure, §§ 74, 90.

"   3............   "   "   "

595,   25.............1865, ch. 357.

596,   29.............1861, ch. 221; 1862, ch. 485.

599,   Head note......1860, ch. 173. As to married women,
            1864, ch. 219.

"   1st sentence of
            foot note......38 Barb. S. C. R. 94.

"   2d sentence of
            foot note.....Not repealed, 42 Barb. S. C. R. 304;
            41 N. Y. R. 425.

600,   3.............1864, ch. 219.

602,   Head note......Referees' fees on sales, 1869, ch. 569.

626,   Top of page.....Not to abate by death of party; judg't
            against substituted deft., 1865, ch. 357.

637,   2.............1869, ch. 807.

638,   Head note......Satisfaction in other counties, 1860,
            ch. 6.

643,   Top of page.....Ex'ns against person on judg'ts of
            female employees, N. Y. city, 1867, ch. 516.

644,   Head note.. ...Seizures by overseers of poor, 1862,
            ch. 473.

645,   22.............1860, ch. 152.

646,   Top of page ....No property exempt on ex'n on judg't
            under $15, in favor of female employee in N. Y.
            city, 1867, ch. 516.

Page.	Section.
646,	Subdivision 2....Pay, &c. of soldiers, 1864, ch. 578.
"	23.............1859, ch. 134; 1866, ch. 782.
657,	91..............1867, ch. 116.
668,	Title I, head n..1865, ch. 357.
675,	Head note......1862, ch. 375.
677,	Head note......Affdts. made in other States and Territories, 1869, ch. 133.
678,	25, Subd. 2.....1865, ch. 421; also as to consul at Paris.
"	26.............As to Canada, 1868 ch. 596.
679,	34.............As to vessels in office of Collector of Customs, 1862, ch. 251.
680,	Head note......1867, ch. 68.
"	39.............Dist. Ct. Justice, N. Y. city, 1857, ch. 344, § 77.
686,	Head note......Of sales and hypothecation of vessels, 1862, ch. 251; 1865, ch. 512.
687,	81.............Or in other States, 1861, ch. 12; 1864, ch. 311; 1871, ch. 361.
694,	.............Except N. Y. and Kings Co's, 1861, ch. 210; 1867, ch. 494. As to N. Y. city, 1870, ch. 539; 1872, ch. 59. As to Kings Co., 1866, ch. 821. Petit jurors at County Cts. and Cts. of Sessions, 1861, ch. 8. P. Jurors at County Cts. and Cts. of Sessions in Westch. Co., 1872, ch. 499.
695,	5.............Telegraph operators exempt, 1861, ch. 215; but see 1862, ch. 477.
696,	7.............But see *ante*, Vol. II, 717, 724.
702,	43, 44 ....Commissioner of Jurors, &c., 1862, ch. 378; 1866, ch. 821; 1870, ch. 315; 1871, ch. 744.
703,	48.............1863, ch. 506.
704,	52.............Telegraph operators, 1861, ch. 215; but see 1862, ch. 477. As to N. Y. city, 1870, ch. 539; 1872, ch. 535.
706,	59.............1863, ch. 506.
711,	Foot of page....Additional petit jurors in Circuit and O. and T. except in N. Y. city, 1870, ch. 409. Ditto, omitting the exception as to N. Y., 1871, ch. 16.
715,	107............1870, ch. 409; 1871, ch. 16.
718,	120, 121 ....1861, ch. 210, does not repeal these two sections, but is supplementary thereto, 1867, ch. 494.
721,	5th foot note....Not repealed, 1 Code Rep. 66.

PAGE.   SECTION.

789,   43.............By Special Sessions in N. Y. city, 1859, ch. 491.

790,   46.............1861, ch. 333.

791,   Top of page.....Dower; sale of real estate, 1870, ch. 717.

792,   Subdivision 1...1869, ch. 433.

"   Subdivision 3...   "

793,   16.............   "

"   Foot of page....Appeal; no stay; when a preferred case, 1869, ch. 433.

795,   Art. 1st, head n..1859, ch. 79; 1860, chs. 208, 469; 1862, ch. 482; 1863, ch. 422.

802,   Head note......On R. R. bridges and trestle work, 1870, ch. 529. On wharves, bridges, &c., 1872, ch. 669.

804,   2d foot note.,...This act repealed, at least as to Buffalo, 1871, ch. 872, §§ 11, 12.

812,   82.............1863, ch. 500; 1866, ch. 752; 1868, ch. 79.

815,   102............As to Rensselaer, 1870, ch. 194.

818,   116............As to Kings and Queens Co.'s, 1862, ch. 478.

820,   125............1869, ch. 558.

821,   128............   "

825,   144............1871, ch. 188.

828,   162............Extended to all the counties except Erie, Kings, Queens, N. Y. and Onondaga, 1869, ch. 558; and except Rensselaer, 1870, ch. 194. Extended to Erie Co., 1872, ch. 691.

"   164............1867, ch. 856; 1870, ch. 385.

834,   18.............Not Marine C't, 1870, ch. 582.

835,   Head note......1868, ch. 828. As to N. Y. city, 1863, ch. 189. District C't, Justices N. Y. city, 1857, ch. 344, § 77. As to bawdy houses, 1868, ch. 764.

837,   '30.............As to N. Y. and Kings Co.'s, 1866, ch. 754.

838,   36.............1862, ch. 368.

845,   Head note...... *Vide* Code of Procedure, § 471.

859,   Head note......As to surplus, 1868, ch. 804; 1870, ch. 706.

862,   Head note......27 N. Y. R. 306. Unconstitutional as it existed in 1868, 5 Barb. S. C. R. 474; 1871, ch. 303.

6

PAGE. SECTION.

862, Foot of page....1869, ch. 888 ; 1870, ch. 38. Westch. Co. exempted from laws of 1868, ch. 888. Proceedings in Westch. Co. to be under Rev. Stat. and amend'ts, 1871, ch. 43. Eastchester, Westch. Co., 1871, ch. 882.

863, Top of page....Staten and Long Isl'ds, 1868, ch. 864 ; 1869, ch. 282 ; 1872, ch. 574.

873, Top of page.....Change of corporation name, 1870, ch. 322.

" Head note......1860, ch. 80.

874, " ......On express Co.'s, 1864, ch. 411.

906, 27............. *Vide*, 1871, ch. 610, § 27.

914, 8.............1859, ch. 496. As to Kings and Westch. Co.'s, 1866, ch. 498.

916, 11.............1860, ch. 493.

" 12............ " ; 1861, ch. 11 ; 1866, ch. 692.

917, Foot of page....Fees of Cl'k of Kings Co., 1865, ch. 713 ; 1867, ch. 128 ; 1868, ch. 720 ; 1871, ch. 374.

919, 22.............1864, ch. 420. No fees where inventory shows less than $500 ; or for apptg. guardian to procure bounty, &c., 1863, ch. 362. All his fees abolished, 1867, ch. 782. Fees abolished except in N. Y. city, 1869, ch. 246. Surrog. Clks. fees, except in N. Y. city, 1869, ch. 246.

922, 27, 2d paragraph.1858, ch. 176 ; 1860, ch. 136 ; 1864, ch. 545 ; 1866, ch. 307.

" 27, 5th paragraph.As to N. Y. city, 1870, ch. 539.

924, 33.............Except as to N. Y., Kings and Westch. Co.'s, 1871, ch. 415 ; 1872, ch. 26. As to N. Y. city, 1869, ch. 569.

925, Top of page.....For confining civil prisoners in Kings Co., 1869, ch. 813.

927, 38.............In N. Y. city, 1868, ch. 565.

" 39.............1869, ch. 820.

" 39, 8th paragraph.As to Westch. Co., 1860, ch. 427. As to Westch. and Kings Co.'s, 1866, ch. 707.

928, 41.............1859, ch. 170 ; 1865, ch. 356.

" 43.............1859, ch. 252.

929, 45............. " ; 1869, ch. 831.

935, Head note......1860, ch. 410 ; 1861, ch. 303 ; 1862, ch. 197.

PAGE.   SECTION.

986,   18.............1865, ch. 172.

"   19............Misconduct of inmates, 1861, ch. 306.

987,   Top of page ....School ship for juvenile delinquents, 1869, ch. 285.

988,   33........ ....Juveniles exempted, 1872, ch. 113.

990,   Ch. II, head n...Accused may testify, 1869, ch. 678.

"   Title I, head n..1862, ch. 374.

991,   1.............District Court Justices, N. Y. city, 1857, ch. 344, § 77. Marine Court Justices, N. Y. city, 1813, ch. 86, § 139.

"   1st foot note..... *Vide post*, 993, foot note.

992,   Head note......Police may make certain arrests without warrant, 1864, ch. 403, § 30 ; *vide* also Met. Police Act. Magistrates to file complaints, &c., 1866, ch. 95.

993,   Top of page ....Kings Co., examination by Justice of the Peace, 1863, ch. 174. Accused may testify, 1869, ch. 678.

"   1.............District Court Justices, N. Y. city, 1857, ch. 344, § 77. Marine Court Justices, N. Y. city, 1813, ch. 86, § 139. Special justices and assistants, *vide* note 1.

"   4.............Endorsements; Met. Police District, 1857, ch. 569, §§ 8, 17.

"   Foot of page....Assistant Justices, now District Court Justices, 1857, ch. 344. Special Justices, now Police Justices, 1848, ch. 153, § 12.

"   Foot n., 2d par.. *Vide* Met. Police Act.

994,   7, 8, 9.........Met. Police District, 1864, ch. 403, § 28.

997,   Subdivision 3...Special justices, now police justices, 1848, ch. 153. Assistant justices, now district court justices, 1852, ch. 324, § 1. As to Marine Court justices, 1813, ch. 86, § 139 ; 1819, ch. 71; but see *ante*, Vol. III, p. 993, § 1.

"   Foot of page....N. Y. city ; bail before magistrate, 1860, ch. 508; Bkln.; bail on Sunday, 1866, ch. 84; 1871, ch. 194, § 37.

1000, Top of page.....Accused may be witness for himself, 1869, ch. 678.

"   Art I, head note.1859, ch. 339.

"   Subdivision 3...1872, ch. 530.

PAGE. SECTION.

1001, Top of page.....As to malicious mischief, 1866, ch. 467.
As to unlawful taking of oysters, 1866, ch. 753.

1006, 25 to 32........Rpld. 1859, ch. 339.

" 27.............Return fee on *certiorari*, 1860, ch. 493;
1866, ch. 692.

1007, 33 to 42........Rpld. 1859, ch. 339.

1008, Top of page.....Title iii, art. 4th, ch. ii, part iv, R. S.
revived, substituting Supreme Court for Court of
Sessions, 1859, ch. 339.

" Head note......1859, ch. 491.

1009, 50.............1857, ch. 446; 1858, ch. 282; 1871,
chs. 302, 438.

" 52.............1859,.ch. 339.

" Foot of page....Any proceeding before two police justices in N. Y. city may now be had before one,
1860, ch. 508. Board of police justices N. Y. city,
1860, ch. 508.

1010, 61.............1863, ch. 404; 1864, ch. 341; 1866,
ch. 692. And see, 1860, ch. 493, § 4. In N. Y.
city to wardens of prisons, 1859, ch. 491; 1867, ch.
961.

1011, 66.............Witnesses in Special Sessions, N. Y.
city, 1859, ch. 491.

" Foot of page....Filing record of conviction; paying
over fines, except in certain cities, 1860, ch. 493.
Ditto, without exception, 1866, ch. 692.

1012, Art. 4th, head n.Article Fourth revived and modified,
1859, ch. 339. Writ of *certiorari* recognized, 1860,
ch. 493; 1866, ch. 692.

" Art. 1st, head n.As to N. Y. city, 1870, ch. 539.

1017, Head note......Indictments for offences against joint
stock Co.'s, 1862, ch. 151.

" 37.............1860, ch. 271.

" Foot of page....Power of Oyer and Terminer to change
place of trial, 1859, ch. 462.

1018, 43.............In Met. Police District, 1869, ch. 278.

" 44.............1860, ch. 431.

1021, 69.............Court may allow fees, 1869, ch. 155.
As to Special Sessions, N. Y. city, 1859, ch. 491.

1025, Top of page..... *Vide ante*, Vol. III, 297, 303.

" Foot of page....Circuit Courts may try indictments
sent from O. & T., 1859, ch. 462. Oyer and Ter-.

PAGE.   SECTION.
miner may send indictments to other counties, 1859 ch. 462.
1027, Top of page.....Accused may be witness for himself, 1869, ch. 678.
"   9...........:....In capital cases, 1872, ch. 475.
1028, 23...........'.....1872, ch. 56.
1029, Foot of page....Judg'ts on trial by Circuit Cts. of indictments removed from O. and T., 1859, ch. 462.
1030, 35.............In capital cases, 1872, ch. 475.
1031, 4.............1860, ch. 135.
1032, 7.............   "
"   8.............1867, ch. 604.
1033, Head note......Certiorari to Special Sessions, 1859, ch. 339.
"   Foot of page....Bills of exceptions, after expiration of judge's term, 1872, ch. 56.
1035, 26....:.........1863, ch. 226. Remittitur from Supreme Court to Oyer and Terminer, 1859, ch. 462.
1036, Art. 1st, head n..In N. Y. city, 1871, ch. 462. Justices of the peace may act in certain cases, 1864, ch. 379.
1039, Foot of page....Records as to minors, 1869, ch. 411.
1040, 31.............1867, ch. 333. In N. Y. city, 1860, ch. 508.
1041, 37.............In Met. Police District, 1860, ch. 259, § 68.
1043, 55.............1861, ch. 97; 1866, ch. 723; 1867, ch. 604.
"   56.............1861, ch. 97; 1866, ch. 723; 1867, ch. 604.
1044, Top of page.....Criminal record to be kept by courts in N. Y. city, 1860, ch. 508; 1867, ch. 961.
"   58.............1861, ch. 97.
1045, 60.............1864, ch. 202; 1867, ch. 604.
"   1.............1866, ch. 692.
"   Foot of page....Associate justice in criminal or bastardy case, $2 per day, 1862, ch. 372.
1046, Top of page.....Justices of Sessions, 1859, ch. 496. Justices of Sessions, Westch. and Kings Co.'s, 1866, ch. 498. Justices of Sessions, Kings Co., 1869, ch. 730.
"   2.............1866, ch. 692.
"   4.............1866, ch. 692; 1869, ch. 820.   .

PAGE. SECTION.

1050, 17, 5th paragraph. 1859, ch. 254.
" Foot of page.... On commitments by police justices in
N. Y. city, 1869, ch. 569.
1066, Title II, head n.. 1860, ch. 399; 1865, ch. 600.
" Foot of page.... Reformatory at Elmira, 1870, ch. 427.
1067, Top of page .... Compensation of officers, 1864, ch.
300; 1865, ch. 600; 1867, ch. 426; 1870, ch. 109.
" Head note...... Keeper to give bond, 1863, ch. 465.
Duties of Inspectors, Agents, and Wardens, 1866,
ch. 458.
1069, Top of page.... Inspectors to employ convicts, 1866,
ch. 458.
1077, Subdivisions 8, 9. 1860, ch. 283.
" 60............. 1862, ch. 417; 1863, ch. 415.
" 61............. " "
1078, 65............. 1862, ch. 403.
1086, Head note...... 1862, ch. 417; 1863, chs. 415, 465;
1866, chs. 330, 458.
· 1087, Top of page .... Iron manufacture at Clinton Prison,
1865, ch. 43; 1866, ch. 72.
" Foot of page.... Quarries at Sing Sing Prison, 1868,
ch. 612.
1089, Top of page..... Examination as to sanity of prisoners,
1869, ch. 895; 1871, ch. 666.
" Head note...... Commutation of term, 1862, ch. 417;
1863, ch. 415; 1864, ch. 321.
" Foot of page.... Tortures in jails abolished, and their
infliction a misdemeanor, 1869, ch. 869.
1091, 2d foot note..... 1865, ch. 353; 1867, ch. 113.
1093, 123...... ..... " "
1097, 156............. 1872, ch. 782.
1099, Foot of page.... Disinfectants in prisons, 1868, ch. 599.
1104, Foot of page.... Fees charged to visitors at prisons,
1862, ch. 417; 1863, ch. 415.
1121, Top of page..... ANIMALS, preservation of health of,
for human food, 1866, ch. 560.
ANIMALS, preservation from Rinder-
pest, 1866, ch. 740; 1867, ch. 453; 1869, ch. 271.
ANIMALS having infectious diseases,
regulation of, 1866, ch. 740; 1867, ch. 453.
1134, Top of page..... BARRELS: Apple, pear, and potato,
1862, ch. 178.

379; 1870, ch. 382, § 2, and ch. 383, § 17; *vide* also 1859, ch. 262, and 1869, ch. 876, § 14.

ELECTIONS in N. Y. city, 1870, ch. 138; 1871, ch. 572; 1872, ch. 570.

1275, Foot of page.... FIRE MARSHAL, 1868, ch. 563; 1871, ch. 584.

Marshals [formerly Constables], 1862, ch. 484; 1864, ch. 569; 1865, ch. 400; 1867, ch. 909; 1871, ch. 804.

1276, Top of page .... CHARTER of N. Y. city amended, 1868, ch. 887.

NEW CHARTER of N. Y. city, 1870, chs. 137, 382, 383; 1871, chs. 573, 574, 583; 1872, chs. 444, 473, 514, 675, 738.

SUPERVISORS, N. Y. city, 1870, chs. 190, 382, 383; 1872, ch. 860.

" Foot of page.... BUREAU OF LICENSES, in N. Y. city, 1863, ch. 231.

Market Companies in N. Y. city, 1871, ch. 820.

1277, Top of page .... Department of Public Charities, &c., N. Y. city, 1860, ch. 510; 1864, ch. 586; 1866, ch. 242; 1869, ch. 238; 1871, ch. 607.

CORPORATION ATTORNEY, N. Y. city, 1871, ch. 724.

" Foot of page.... Surrogate of N. Y. city, his rights, duties, &c., 1870, ch. 359.

1284, Top of page .... PARKS, private, 1871, ch. 831.

" Foot of page.... OYSTERS, unlawful taking of, 1866, ch. 753.

1285, Foot of page.... PASSENGERS, sick or indigent, 1866, ch. 737.

1287, Top of page .... PENDENCY OF ACTION, notices of, to be recorded, 1864, ch. 53.

1288, Top of page .... Petroleum, storage of, 1865, ch. 773; 1866, ch. 872.

1289, Top of page .... POLICE COURTS in N. Y. city, records of, 1867, ch. 961.

" Foot of page.... Railroad police, 1863, ch. 346. Steamboat police, 1866, ch. 259.

POLICE at agricultural fairs, 1859, ch. 36; 1862, ch. 284; 1869, ch. 326.

POLICE at State Inebriate Asylum, 1866, ch. 673.

ERRATA

Noticed in Fifth Edition R. S.

VOL. I.

Page.	Section.			
390,	..............The side notes except one are higher than their proper places.			
395,	...............The number of the Title omitted.			
399,	Line 6 ....Substitute t for i, and *dele* t.			
404,	2..............For *lietenant* read *lieutenant*.			
422,	Side note....... " *ŋotic* " notice.			
431,	27............. " proceeeings " proceedings.			
445,	16 .... " withiout " without.			
456,	Note.......... " secreary " secretary.			
469,	13............. " defsnse " defense.			
506,	Line 4 .... " attoreny " attorney.			
621,	Line 66 .... " consforming " conforming.			
677,	Line 6 .... " orther " other.			
795,	112............ " day " days.			
817,	8, subd. 3 ...... " beween " between.			
883,	Line 28 .... " .Dstrict " District.			
"	202............ " offiénses " offenses.			
884,	205............ " reciepts " receipts.			
	208, side note...After attorney, add—Albany.			
914,	30............For tows read towns.			
" "	30............ " agregate " aggregate.			
930,	Line 14 .... " to " by.			

VOL. II.

PAGE.	SECTION.			
19,	Head'g top of p. For Emigration	read	Health.	
143,	Subdivision 2... "	puplic	"	public.
415,	183........... "	pupose	"	purpose.
421,	Line 54 .... "	pelalty	"	penalty.
426,	Line 1 .... "	ditected	"	directed.
468,	Line 26 .... "	undermaking	"	undermarking.
609,	Side note....... "	trustes	"	trustees.
632,	25............. "	ceneteries	"	cemeteries.
717,	63............. "	fifty	"	fifth.

VOL. III.

19,	69............. For eccleciastical read ecclesiastical.	
29,	Head'g top of p. " of " by.	
30,	" .. " of " by.	
38,	Head note...... " devises " devisees.	
54,	43............. This should be numbered 42.	
64,	20............. For partnerhsip read partnership	
65,	24, side note.... " appliaation " application.	
85,	Line 2 .... " stat— " stating.	
110,	9, side note..... " dates " states.	
207,	9............. " 1489 " 1849.	
238,	Foot note ...... " revisors " revisers.	
282,	20............. *Dele* 280.	
310,	Head'g top of p..Add—General Sessions, N. Y. city.	
311,	" ..Add—General and Special Sessions and Oyer and Terminer.	
312,	Head'g top of p..Strike out—Common Pleas, and insert in lieu thereof—General Sessions, N. Y. Add—City Judge & Recorder, N. Y.	
313,	Head'g top of p..Add—Court of Common Pleas, before the words—of the city of New York.	
314,	Head'g top of p..Strike out Court of Common Pleas, and insert in place thereof—Justices of Sessions,	

PAGE.   SECTION.

Albany, Kings, Columbia, and Erie counties; Brooklyn local courts; Pay of additional Supreme Court Judge, 1st District.

315,   Head'g top of p..Add—Justices of the Peace, Suffolk county; City Judge & Recorder, N. Y. city.

348, ...After heading, Title VII, strike out the words—Of the city court of Brooklyn, and insert in place thereof the words—Of courts in the city of Brooklyn.

352,   Head'g top of p..Add—Police Justice, Brooklyn.

353,   "   ..Strike out City Court, and insert in place thereof—Justices of the Peace and Police Justices.

380,   Line 32 ....For contr   read court.

381,   Head note, line 1. " court   " courts.

"   "   line 9. " counselor " counselors.

452, ...The tenth paragraph should be the seventh.

660,   2.............For defendent read defendant.

"   4............. " defendent " defendant.

777,   Head'g top of p..After Suits, insert the words—by and.

"   Head note, line 1. " Of actions, "   " —by and.

825,   Head'g top of p.. " Art. add figure 2.

837,   31.............For suffrance read sufferance.

914,   9, 8th paragraph. " taking   " taxing.

940,   9............. " prescribed " prescribe.

944,   37.............After—age, insert the word—of.

957,   63.............For by   read buy.

973,   11............ " guiliy " guilty.

"   15, side note ....Before malicious add the words— wilful and.

985, ...The figure 5 is omitted in the page number.

992,   10.............For cognizance read recognizance.

993,   Foot note.......The words—"special justices and assistant justices" have not been inserted in the text.

1036,   1, side note .....For reduced   read summoned.

1050,   17............. " convcit   " convict.

1074,   Subdivision 3... " treament   " treatment.

9

PAGE.   SECTION.

1101, Head'g top of p..After State, insert the words—and
         county.
1103, Head'g top of p..After State, insert the words—and
         county.
1211, Line 64 ....For apfirmations read affirmations.
1221, Line 34 .... " 457   " 455.
1232, ...Strike out lines 22 to 41 right hand
         column, beginning with the words, "IDIOTS,
         LUNATICS," and ending with [See State Lunatic
         Asylum]," and insert in lieu thereof the word
         "IDIOTS."

www.ingramcontent.com/pod-product-compliance
Lightning Source LLC
Chambersburg PA
CBHW021536270326

41930CB00008B/1276